SEVEN FIGURE
AMI$H

FROM BUGGY TO BENZ

COMPANION WORKBOOK

BY AMOS BORNTREGER

WITH MYRA MILLER, PhD

BookWise Publishing
Riverton, Utah
www.bookwisepublishing.com

Additional copies of this book may be found at www.amosborntreger.com.

With Myra Miller, PhD
Co-Author: Tina Sterling
Editor: Jane Roth
Illustrator: Ken Miller
Cover Design: Courtney Mellinger and
Francine Platt, Eden Graphics, Inc.
Interior Design: Francine Platt, Eden Graphics, Inc.

Library of Congress Data: Pending

ISBN: 978-1-60645-157-1

First Edition: 2016

10 9 8 7 6 5 4 3 2 1

Printed in the United States of America

Introduction

Seven Figure Ami$h shares my personal story. It is how I went from worrying about paying the bills and caring for my family to attaining financial freedom for myself and others.

I hope that from it you will draw on the lessons I learned—through my own experiences and from the experiences of others. I want those lessons to help you achieve the success and happiness you dream of for yourself.

The *Seven Figure Ami$h: From Buggy to Benz Companion Workbook* takes those stories/lessons and presents them with a method to learn what I learned on the road to success. It offers a series of questions to guide you through the process.

I have included activities to build on the qualities, skills, and experiences I believe are most helpful in fulfilling your dreams. Many people have self-imposed barriers. Barriers are symptoms of our thinking. However, moving forward and getting what you want out of life is about figuring out the barriers that are blocking your success, confronting them head-on, and then designing your life. The more you resist the barriers, the more they are likely to persist.

My most compelling barrier was deciding whether or not to leave the Amish community. I knew there would be consequences. I knew the pain would be almost unbearable. But realizing that breaking free from this barrier would open the door to relieving some of my hardships and be the best way to happiness and success for my family, I knew I had to let go of my fear and do it anyway.

NOTES

DISSOLVING BARRIERS AND MOVING FORWARD

Through my own experiences and in working with others, I have developed a list of barriers that I find are common:

- **Ego.** Sometimes those around us, and the messages we send ourselves, tell us we have to be perfect. Nonsense! No one is perfect. We are not designed to be perfect. We are human. Perfectionism is often about believing that if we can just do something perfectly, other people will love us and accept us. We believe that if we are not perfect, we will never be good enough. Again, nonsense! Just relax. Try to do your best. The rest will follow.

- **Knowledge.** We often believe we have to know more—be more educated, have more experience—before we can try something different.

- **Fear.** Overcoming fear doesn't happen overnight. It is a process. When it comes to making a living, the fear of risk can raise its ugly head. Having the life you want involves taking risk. Fear has to be confronted. The fear goes away when we take action toward those things that frighten us. Getting rid of fear happens when we stop telling ourselves we have to know everything to do something well. Often people do not realize fear is holding them back. It prevents moving forward. It causes paralysis.

- **Time.** Time is frequently used as a reason to hesitate in taking a step forward or in a new direction. Many times it is not utilized wisely.

- **Self-confidence.** Self-confidence is a big one. Having confidence in ourselves is important in almost every aspect of our lives, yet many people struggle with this. Confident people inspire confidence in others. Gaining self-confidence is one of the ways people find success. It can be learned. And we can build it higher. Be cautious of becoming over confident, however. This can be interpreted as arrogance.

- **Procrastination.** People who procrastinate put things off to the last minute. This can be a problem in both your personal and professional life. You may miss opportunities, experience high stress, or feel guilty. Do not procrastinate on the big things by focusing on the things that are small distractions.

- **Blame.** Blame usually occurs when we feel badly about something, and we want to get rid of the bad feeling. "They didn't teach me enough . . .. It was not clear to me . . .. I didn't understand." Just like the law of attraction, when you focus on the negative, the negative happens. When focused on the positive, the positive happens.

- **Money.** "I don't have enough money to do this." Most of us don't. Money can work for us. We have to follow our passion; the money will follow. Follow your goals with a clear focus.

I know many people, including myself, who have faced those barriers and achieved more than they ever dreamed possible. They have done this by facing their perceived barriers head on and letting go of them.

Dissolving Barriers and Moving Forward Worksheet

In this lesson, you will begin to uncover the things that are holding you back—the things that are creating barriers to moving forward. It is important to take time to really reflect on your answers. Then, list the steps you need to make in order to take action.

1. What is the biggest barrier you believe you need to overcome to move forward?

2. What are you telling yourself that creates this barrier?

3. What do you need in order to change your thinking?

4. List the action steps you will take to overcome your barrier.

5. Give yourself a time-line for addressing your action steps. It can be less time or more time. It is what works best for you.

NOTES

Setting Goals and Eliminating Hesitation

Dreams rarely become reality without first clearly deciding what you want for yourself and then setting goals to get there. As I embarked on my journey to find what was right for me, I learned that setting goals was my key to motivation. Writing those goals down was the first step toward getting me where I wanted to be. I created a dream board. Setting goals helped organize my time and focus my resources. Success!

Many people feel they are working hard but getting nowhere. Often, this is a result of not spending enough time thinking about what they really want—thinking about their long-term vision. Ask yourself, "What do you want from life over the next ten years?" You need focus. To achieve what you want, you must first be clear about your vision for the future. Know why you want this. If you are clear about the reason, the goal is easier to achieve.

Successful people break their long-term goals into smaller goals—what they want to achieve in the next five years, next year, next month, next week, and today. It is helpful to categorize ideas. Decide what you want to achieve in areas such as your career, finances, your family, and education. Put your goals on paper. Then the objective is to start creating a plan to move forward.

Be sure to create a daily checklist of the things you can do today to work toward your goals. Review your To-Do list on a daily basis and check it against your goals. If it is not something that helps you achieve your goals, question whether it needs to be on the list.

You *must* write down your goals. This alone will help you to learn what knowledge is needed. It helps you organize your time and resources.

My own experience has taught me this:

- Deciding what I want without worrying about obstacles helps me be more clear with myself. I had to *believe* I could overcome the obstacles.

- I had to define the *purpose* of my goal. I had to know *why* this was important to me.

- It takes as much energy to think about *not* having money as it does to focus on *having* money. Focus on the positive.

- I had to spend time reflecting on the barriers that were getting in my way, such as thinking there was an obstacle I could not overcome.

- Nothing will happen unless I put my ideas and goals on paper. Writing down my goals increases my chances of success.

- I had to have a clear time-line.

- I had to look at my weaknesses, not as things that would get in the way, but things that could become my strengths.

- I had to get outside my comfort zone. I was shy and introverted, therefore I was afraid to speak on stage. But because I allowed myself to go outside my comfort zone, I am now passionate about speaking and sharing lessons I have learned along the way.

- The only way to get where I wanted to be meant moving forward without hesitation.

Goals are more achievable when using the S.M.A.R.T. Method.

- **S** – Make your goals specific. Rather than, "I want to take a trip in the next five years," state, "I want to visit Pennsylvania by the year 2018." Be positive. Rather than saying, "Don't do a poor job," say, "Do this well."

- **M** – Make sure your goals are measurable and meaningful. "How will I know when I have achieved my goal?" Focus on being precise with your goals.

- **A** – Make sure your goals are achievable. Are your goals action-oriented? Set priorities to avoid feeling overwhelmed.

- **R** – Make sure your goals are relevant and rewarding.

- **T** – Make sure your goals have a time-line, and you can *track* them. "I can place a check mark next to this because I have completed the task."

Setting Goals and Eliminating Hesitation
Worksheet

In this lesson, you will define your goals and map out the steps needed to achieve those goals. This is your road map for achieving what you want to achieve.

1. What is my lifetime goal?

2. What obstacles do I need to overcome to achieve my goal?

3. What steps can I take to overcome my obstacles?

4. What are my goals for each category of my life (i.e., career, family, health)?

5. If I am to achieve my overall goal, what do I need to do in the next five years, one year, month, week, or day to work toward that goal?

6. What is my daily "To-Do" list?

5-Year goal To-Do_____

1-Week goal To-Do_____

1-Year goal To-Do_____

Daily goal To-Do_____

1-Month goal To-Do_____

NOTES

LESSON 3

ACTIVE LISTENING AND LEARNING LESSONS

"Listen to understand and not to reply."

– AMOS

Active listening, ongoing learning, and developing the skill set needed to achieve your goals are essential to success. I learned this early on. Growing up Amish, my education, in large part, was based on life experiences. I learned that by asking questions and listening to others I would get further ahead and make fewer mistakes in the process.

Later in life, I learned that, if I paid close attention to the right people and really listened, it would go a greater way toward reaching my goals. I spend 75% of my time listening and 25% talking.

As I talk about in my book, *Seven Figure Ami$h*, during one of my trips, I decided to stop and check in on my business partner. Sometimes just showing up and letting someone know you are there for support is half the battle. I concentrated on listening to his words . . . I made sure I had good eye contact and that I struck a soft and deliberate tone. I gave him a few tips and reminded him of some techniques that I thought would help. In that brief twenty minutes, my business partner knew I was there to support him.

Listening is one of the most important skills you can cultivate. How well you listen affects the quality of your relationship with others. It can have a major impact on how effective you are at your work

Good listening skills can lead to better customer satisfaction. Listening and the openness to learn can lead to greater productivity and making fewer mistakes. Many successful people credit their success to effective listening.

A good listener is not only good at listening to what is being said, but pays attention to body language and notices inconsistencies between verbal and non-verbal communication.

We all want to be heard, and we want others to listen to us.

You can become a more active and better listener. These techniques will help ensure that you are listening to the other person and that the other person knows you are hearing what they are saying.

- Show you are listening by continually making eye contact with the person talking to you.

- Avoid being distracted by everything else around you.

- Make sure your body language and gestures communicate that you are listening. Nod occasionally, smile when appropriate, and make sure your posture is open and inviting.

- Let the other person know you are really listening by paraphrasing what has been said. Reflect back, "What I'm hearing is," and "I understand you to say."

- Ask questions to clarify points. "I'm hearing this. Is this what you mean?"

- Never interrupt the person talking.

- Always treat the other person the way you would want to be treated. Listen with respect and understanding.

In today's high tech world, communication is more important than ever. Genuine listening has become rare. Yet it is the key to building relationships, solving problems, and gaining knowledge and understanding.

The subconscious mind turns off and we lose people when we listen to simply reply rather than listening to understand. Listening 75% of the time gives us the proper connection and preparation to have the right information available in order to be helpful.

Active Listening and Learning Lessons
Worksheet

In this lesson, you will be guided through a series of questions or activities that will help you to improve your listening skills. You will become more aware of how well you listen and begin to uncover areas where more work is required.

The next time you have an opportunity to listen or you are aware of focusing on listening, ask yourself these questions.

1. Did I maintain eye contact with the speaker?

2. Was I present and paying attention to what the speaker was saying?

3. Was I non-judgmental, and listening with an open mind?

4. Did I feel compelled to interrupt the speaker, or did I wait for the speaker to pause before asking a clarifying question?

5. Use a journal, notepad, or computer to write about your experience. Focus on the skills you applied well, and note which skills will require more work.

Repeat this process over and over. Eventually, effective listening will become second nature.

NOTES

Leading a Team and Motivating People

The ability to lead and motivate people is critical to success. Teams count on strong leadership. They turn to leadership to solve problems, navigate through change, or to make tough decisions. Teams look for a good leader to help them achieve their goals.

I've learned many lessons that I now share with my team by connecting with leaders who have gone through pain and struggles to reach their goals. Because they have willingly had the courage to share their stories, I've benefited by learning through their experiences and have avoided making the same mistakes.

I surround myself with leaders who still consider themselves in the learning process. They are people who are on a continual path of self-improvement. They recognize the value of continual personal and professional growth to better themselves and to share lessons learned with those around them.

No one achieves success alone. Success is achieved when you are surrounded by people who support your efforts to meet your goals.

There are many traits and qualities that are recognized as signs of a great leader. But know, however, there is no magic combination of characteristics that makes a leader successful. The key is to understand as much about leadership as you can and determine the approach that works best for your situation. You have to know yourself.

As I have worked to be a good leader, I believe the following qualities, or traits, are important.

- **Adaptability**
- **Empathy**
- **Understanding**
- **Humility**
- **Effective Listening**
- **Honesty**
- **Effective Communication**
- **Confidence**
- **Commitment**
- **A Positive Attitude**

As a team leader, it is your job to inspire and motivate your team.

True leaders use their power and experience in a positive way to motivate others. They recognize that motivated team members produce more and that with energy and enthusiasm, they are far more effective.

People can have all the experience in the world, but unless they are motivated, they are unlikely to achieve their true potential. Work does not seem like work when people are motivated and excited about what they do.

It is hard to motivate people without first understanding what motivates them. Are they motivated most by money? By recognition for their hard work and accomplishments? What motivates a person? What motivates *you*?

Leading a Team and Motivating People
Worksheet

In this lesson, you will be guided through a series of questions or activities that will help you identify your strengths and weaknesses as they relate to team building and motivating people. This exercise will help to uncover areas that need work to be more effective in building teams and leading people.

1. What do you believe to be your greatest strengths as a leader?

2. What do you believe to be your greatest weaknesses as a leader?

3. Find two books you could read on leadership. Read those books, then list lessons learned.

4. Practice the things that make you uncomfortable with a friend or mentor. Ask your friend or mentor to provide feedback about your interaction.

5. Write down the names of ten people you feel that, either by building or growing upon your relationship, you would benefit. Then reach out to those people and ask for a meeting to connect.

6. Write down what motivates you.

7. Talk to your team members. Ask them to share their goals, values, and aspirations.

NOTES

Managing Time and Getting Things Done

Life is made up of seeds of time. Every minute of the day is a seed. Spending my time wisely and efficiently better ensures I reap the harvest.

Every day, I reflect on how I have spent my time. I ask myself whether how I spent my time aligns with my goals and whether it will lead to the greatest chance of success.

In today's culture, we often become overwhelmed with tasks that have to be managed as part of our working day. To get this out of our minds, we need to write our tasks down, either on paper or electronically. This way we can stop feeling overwhelmed and start feeling more in control.

Next, task lists should be organized. There are many ways to do this, and there is no right or wrong approach. For example, you may choose to organize your task list by:

- **Actionable**

- **Reading/Education**

- **Project Planning**

Take some time to reflect on your task list. Be sure to break the list into easily digestible steps. Which tasks can you successfully handle, and which tasks could be delegated to someone else?

The next step in the process is to take action. Develop a system for controlling your daily tasks. Each task should have a deadline. It is important to think about how much time might be needed to complete each task. Prioritizing tasks is important. Your task list may need further refinement.

Taking the time to learn about time management and applying the principles reduces stress, increases productivity and efficiency, may lead to a better professional reputation, and certainly makes achieving goals more attainable.

Failure to manage time efficiently can lead to missed deadlines, poor work quality, higher stress levels, and a poor professional reputation.

"Every minute of the day is a seed to sow."
— AMOS

MindTools®, an online resource for developing essential skills for an excellent career, reveals ten common time management mistakes.

1. **Failing to keep a To-Do list.** Have you ever had that nagging feeling you are forgetting something important? If so, you probably don't use a To-Do list.

2. **Not setting personal goals.** Goal-setting is essential to managing your time well. It gives you a destination and vision to work toward. When you know where you want to go, you can manage your priorities, time, and resources to get there. It will help identify what is worth spending time on and what is a potential distraction.

3. **Not prioritizing.** If you want to manage time better, you have to prioritize.

4. **Failing to manage distractions.** Daily distractions can quickly eat away at your time. To get the most done, you have to manage those distractions.

5. **Procrastination.** To beat procrastination, commit to starting on a project for ten minutes. Use action plans so tasks may be completed in smaller, manageable steps.

6. **Taking on too much**. Sometimes it is important to say "no."

7. **Thriving on busy.** Addiction to busyness rarely means you are effective. Slow down and manage your time better.

8. **Multitasking.** Multitasking can lead to mistakes. Instead, focus on one task at a time. That way you produce higher quality work.

9. **Not taking breaks.** It's okay. Take a break. You'll be more productive.

10. **Ineffectively scheduling tasks.** Know when you are the most productive. Organize your tasks accordingly.

Managing Time and Getting Things Done
Worksheet

In this lesson, you will focus on action steps for developing a process to better manage your time and get things done. It is important to stick to your process. You want to get ahead, rather than fall back into old patterns.

1. Start by re-visiting your long-term and short term goals. Remind yourself of what is important to you to achieve today, tomorrow, and in the future.

2. List all your tasks.

3. Organize your tasks into categories.

4. Create a deadline for each task.

5. Delegate tasks as you deem appropriate.

6. Be sure to add at least two resources (books, online blogs, etc.) to learn more about time management.

NOTES

LESSON 6

MODEL BEHAVIOR AND REPLICATE TRAINING

"Training is the best form of selling."
– AMOS

Equip people with the right tools—a good process and system—and the selling part is easy. In most cases, the product will sell itself. I can tell you, without question, that among the key factors to my success are engaging with the right people and making sure my team has been provided access to knowledge that will help them to do their work well.

Anyone who has ever been asked to do a job for which they have not properly been trained will understand the stress.

Teaching someone to replicate your efforts and do what you do will lead to success. Training is the best form of selling.

There are two areas to consider when training. First, "Am I providing my team with the necessary knowledge and a good system to do their jobs well? Have I equipped them with the technical knowledge needed? Do they understand and are they able to replicate the process?" Second, "Am I a good role model for my team to follow? Have I demonstrated good interpersonal skills, or people skills, that will increase the chances of accomplishing their objectives?"

Good interpersonal skills, or people skills, have as much impact, if not more, on success in selling than technical knowledge. Having good people skills goes beyond an industry. The better your interpersonal skills, the better you will lead your team and succeed at reaching your goals.

These are some of the character traits that would define someone considered to have good interpersonal skills.

- They model the behavior they expect from their team.

- They have a positive attitude and approach problem-solving with a good attitude.

- They never forget to thank the people with whom they work.

- They recognize the importance of good working relationships.

- If a conflict arises, they think about resolving the conflict with respect.

- They are good listeners. They wait for the other person to complete their thought, then they may offer ideas or feedback.

- They will ask questions as a way to engage in a conversation. They demonstrate their interest in having conversations with others by asking questions.

- They demonstrate good manners such as saying, "thank you" for a job well done.

- Their approach to problem-solving is to identify the problem, dissect the problem so it is fully understood, examine all options pertaining to solutions, and find ways to solve the problem. The difference between a good problem-solver and one who is not so good is how they communicate and how they go about solving the problem.

- They are self-confident without being arrogant.

- They manage their time well, respecting the time of others.

Use this list to gauge your skills. Find areas where you want to improve.

Model Behavior and Replicate Training Worksheet

In this lesson, focus on action steps for developing a good mind-set for training your people. Work on your people skills to develop better relationships. Evaluate yourself in the following areas and work on those where you feel the need of improvement. Choose someone you trust to work on these skills with you, and ask for feedback. A good way to practice interpersonal skills is to ask yourself if this is how you would like to be treated by someone else.

1. List all the ways in which you would like to improve your interaction and communication with others.

2. Find someone with whom to have a conversation. Take turns talking about an event from your life. As you listen to your partner, repeat what they have said.

3. Think about a time when a conversation did not go well. How would you handle that conversation differently?

4. Write about a time when you felt you were less than respectful of someone else. What could you do differently to show more respect?

5. Do you approach problem solving with respect for others?

6. Think of a time when you had a conflict with someone else. How could you have handled the situation differently?

NOTES

LESSON 7

FOLLOWING YOUR PASSION AND MAKING MONEY

"Follow your passion and money will follow."
— AMOS

We are happiest when we do work that is meaningful to us—when we are able to make money doing something for which we feel a great deal of passion.

In my book, *Seven Figure Ami$h*, I talk about the many jobs I held to make money. While I enjoyed those jobs, I found myself questioning whether I was working on projects for which I really felt passionate. Once I understood that money often follows passion and spent some time discovering my passion, I was able to realize my dreams. Following my passion has allowed me to do my best work and feel happy in the process.

There are two ways to approach business. You can either create your own dreams or build the dreams and passion of someone else. With multi-level marketing, I found that not only could I build on my dreams, but I could help build the dreams of others. Our passions aligned.

Figuring out what we are most passionate about is the first step toward success and happiness. Many people stay in jobs for years even though they know they want to do something different. But they haven't actually figured out what it is they really want to do. So reach back to your childhood. What are the things that made you feel most alive?

Next, spend time thinking about what you are most curious about. Following your curiosity will help to tap into your uniqueness compared to others. Ask yourself what you would do if money was no object—if money was something that you did not need to worry about. The key to finding your passion is to be open, to explore and to not stop looking. Begin to challenge yourself to do things you have not tried before but might find interesting.

Then begin to think about whether you can turn your passion into money. This requires an open mind. It requires that you apply creativity to your thinking.

When people are doing something they are passionate about, you can see it on their faces. They light up. People want to be around people who are happy. When people are happy, good things happen. Have you ever noticed that when you feel good about things, better things just seem to happen? Good energy attracts good energy.

Passion can lead to money. Surrounding yourself with good people increases your chances.

Money can be generated in two ways. First, you can multiply your money by investing wisely. Second, you can multiply your money by multiplying people. Most people believe that by investing, they will generate money faster. In the multi-level marketing business model, multiplying people actually generates money faster. In addition, it makes money for everyone and everyone benefits—not just the person at the top. This is much simpler and is, hands-down, the best way to generate money.

Build your network. Surround yourself with good people. Build a team. You can only become successful in network marketing if you help others become successful.

Following Your Passion and Making Money
Worksheet

In this lesson, focus on action steps for finding your passion. There are many tools and books on the market that focus on this subject. Take some time to explore them. Then address questions about building your team and making money for everyone. If needed, refer back to your goals in Lesson 1 and building teams in Lesson 4.

1. Thinking back to your childhood, what are the things that made you the happiest?

2. What are some of the things you are most curious about?

3. What do people thank you for?

4. What do you feel really good at?

5. List a person or people from whom you receive inspiration. What is it about them that inspires you?

6. Discuss a time when you were so engaged in something you completely lost track of time.

7. If you could write a book to help the world, what would that book be about?

Now, the people to build your team.

1. List three organizations or networking opportunities that would provide you an opportunity to meet people who could be part of your team.

2. What will you do to teach your team what they need to know to succeed?

3. How will you keep your team motivated?

NOTES

NOTES

NOTES

NOTES

www.ingramcontent.com/pod-product-compliance
Lightning Source LLC
Chambersburg PA
CBHW081307040426
42452CB00014B/2682